soulspark

JOURNAL

An intuitive journal and guided monthly process
to define your desires and manifest your dreams!

Published and distributed by Soul Spark
Copyright © Jessica Louise, 2020
ISBN: 978-0-6450666-5-4

This journal belongs to

Welcome

This book, this process, and this journal is dedicated to you —
you holding these pages in your hands.

No one-word captures the presence that connects us all. As I set this
intention to craft a process to manifest my desires as simply and
effectively as possible, I was led on a path.

Ideas formed. Inspiration here, a quote there, an insight there.
Aha moments occurred. Principles and ideas started to cohesively
fit together. And it grew, it evolved, it transformed into a guided
ongoing manifesting process to:

· To uncover our deep desires

· To deliberately think about things that we want to experience

· To find a way to be a vibrational match to our desires so that we
can receive them

· To find a way to ease our discomfort and eventually transform it
into a feeling of hope, and then positive expectation

· To place ourselves in a vibrational place of receiving all that we're
asking for

· To separate our thoughts away from the past aand what has been
towards our new reality

· To separate our thoughts away from others' experiences and towards our new reality

· To allow ourselves to feel how we'd like to feel now, regardless

· To experience the exhilaration of joyously, consciously, creating our own reality

· To find ways of holding ourselves consistently in vibrational harmony with those desires in order to receive their manifestation

While I was there for the writing of these pages, I cannot take credit for them all. They are a combination: one girl's journey (that'd be mine) lessons learned from teachers and friends, and channelled messages from the universe.

My intention for this journal is to encourage you to connect with your heart, your intuition — and design your desires beyond what you could ever have imagined possible!

Defining the aspects that are important to you, that align with your values and your soul, and magically watching them come to be.

My vision for Soul Spark has always been more than just these pages. Below are some ways that you can take this process further:

Share #soulsparkjournal on Instagram to connect with others using the process too

Visit soulsparkjournal.com/spark-circle and learn about creating your own Spark Circle and share the journey with a sisterhood.

So much love,
Jessica

This is the journal I've always wished I had,
and I'm so excited to share this process with you too!

Let the magic begin ✳

Spark Circle

My vision for the Soul Spark Journal has always been more than just these pages. And a beautiful way to enhance this process is to share this journey alongside others.

Why Create a Spark Circle?

- To seek the support of a sisterhood
- To diminish a feeling of isolation and to bring a sense of community for yourself and others
- To enhance the experience my making meaningful connections
- To dive deeper into the SoulSpark manifesting process
- To share the journey with a group of supportive friends to listen, to validate your feelings and cheer you on!

Spark Circle

Read on for some tips on creating your own Spark Circle:

- Join our online platform exclusively created for our Soul Spark community and express your interest in forming your own Spark Circle by visiting soulsparkjournal.com/spark-circle
- Email your closest friends proposing the Spark Circle idea
- Post on Facebook or Instagram that you're looking for some friends to go through the SoulSpark process with

Your Spark Circle can be as free-flowing or as structured as you like! Some ideas could be:

- Meet weekly and share your thoughts and feelings along the way
- Meet monthly and share how your going with your manifesting
- Get creative and make your Spark Circle your own
- Or make it an excuse just to get together regularly to share and connect with one another

Your circle doesn't have to be in-person.
Any type of virtual circle works, too!

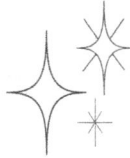

Desire Prompts

The higher vision of this process is to encourage you to connect with
your heart and design your desires beyond what you could have
imagined possible, in ways that excite you,
uplift you and those around you.

Let's stretch our perceptions, let's open ourselves up to the limitless
possibilities and dare to let our true nature shine.

What lights me up?

What is time well spent?

What would I never regret attempting, even if I failed?

What values to do hold close to my heart?

....

....

....

....

....

....

....

....

....

....

....

....

....

....

....

....

....

....

....

....

....

Do I know how I want to live my life? If so, how

What does my inner guidance feel like ...

What really excites me?

....
....
....
....
....
....
....
....
....
....
....
....
....
....
....
....
....
....
....
....
....
....
....
....

If I could do anything, if there was no chance of failure,
if all external judgements went away and I had $100 million
in the bank... What are some things I would like to do?
You've practically just won the lottery and you're magical!

....

....

....

....

....

....

....

....

....

....

....

....

....

....

....

....

....

....

....

What do I crave?

....

....

....

....

....

....

....

....

....

....

....

....

....

....

....

....

....

....

....

....

....

....

How can I have more fun in life?

....

....

....

....

....

....

....

....

....

....

....

....

....

....

....

....

....

....

....

....

....

....

If I gave myself permission to seek out new passions, what would I like to explore?

....

....

....

....

....

....

....

....

....

....

....

....

....

....

....

....

....

....

....

....

....

....

Where is my intuitive guidance leading me?

....

....

....

....

....

....

....

....

Am I onboard, or am I resisting this pathway / opportunity?

....

....

....

....

....

....

....

....

....

....

....

How do I embrace who I really am?

If I allowed myself to feel all that I truely want; without guilt,
judgement or censoring - what do I really want?

....

....

....

....

....

....

....

....

....

For the the world / for the collective?

....

....

....

....

....

....

....

....

....

....

....

....

For my family, friends and my community?

....
....
....
....
....
....
....
....
....
....

For myself?

....
....
....
....
....
....
....
....
....
....
....
....
....

$\diamondplus$

Define Your Desires

FUN
RECREATION
ADVENTURE
EXCITEMENT
VARIETY

MINDSET
PROSPERITY
FUTURE PLANS
SELF CONFIDENCE
FINANCES

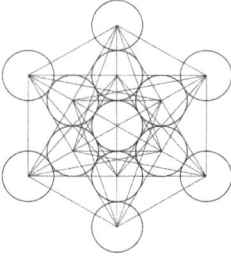

HEALTH
WELLBEING
SELF CARE
SELF LOVE
FITNESS

RITUAL
GROWTH
SPRITUALITY
CONNECTION
FAITH

FRIENDSHIP
CONNECTION
LOVE LIFE
FAMILY
SOCIAL LIFE

STUDY
CAREER
CONTRIBUTION
INNOVATION
BUSINESS

FUN / RECREATION / ADVENTURE / EXCITEMENT / VARIETY

Out of the above categories, I'm most drawn to...

....

... at this point in time. And what I would most like to do or have is ...

What would I like to *have?*

....

....

....

....

....

....

....

What would I like to *experience?*

....

....

....

....

....

....

....

Who would I like to *be?*

....

....

....

....

....

....

....

WELLBEING / SELF CARE / HEALTH / SELF LOVE / FITNESS

Out of the above categories, I'm most drawn to...

....

... at this point in time. And what I would most like to do or have is ...

What would I like to *have?*

....

....

....

....

....

....

....

What would I like to *experience?*

....

....

....

....

....

....

....

Who would I like to *be?*

....

....

....

....

....

....

....

CONNECTION / FRIENDSHIP / FAMILY / LOVE LIFE / SOCIAL LIFE

Out of the above categories, I'm most drawn to...

....

... at this point in time. And what I would most like to do or have is ...

What would I like to *have?*

....
....
....
....
....
....
....

What would I like to *experience?*

....
....
....
....
....
....
....

Who would I like to *be?*

....
....
....
....
....
....
....

INNOVATION / STUDY / CAREER / BUSINESS / CONTRIBUTION

Out of the above categories, I'm most drawn to...

....

... at this point in time. And what I would most like to do or have is ...

What would I like to *have?*

....
....
....
....
....
....
....

What would I like to *experience?*

....
....
....
....
....
....
....

Who would I like to *be?*

....
....
....
....
....
....
....

PERSONAL GROWTH / SPIRITUALITY / FAITH / RITUAL / CONNECTION

Out of the above categories, I'm most drawn to...

....

... at this point in time. And what I would most like to do or have is ...

What would I like to *have?*

....

....

....

....

....

....

....

What would I like to *experience?*

....

....

....

....

....

....

....

Who would I like to *be?*

....

....

....

....

....

....

....

PROSPERITY / FINANCES / FUTURE PLANS / MINDSET / SELF CONFIDENCE

Out of the above categories, I'm most drawn to...

....

... at this point in time. And what I would most like to do or have is ...

What would I like to *have?*

....
....
....
....
....
....
....

What would I like to *experience?*

....
....
....
....
....
....
....

Who would I like to *be?*

....
....
....
....
....
....
....

Guided Process

Many beautiful publications have been written, and workshops offered on the law of attraction. The aim of this guided process is to allow you to experience a powerful way to consistently integrate the practice of the Law of Attraction into your life - to help you to tune in to the vibration of your desires so that they can be received!

The Soul Spark guided process consists of selecting one singular desire and focusing on it for that particular month - something you would love to be, do or have.

Each week we build upon the last, opening our hearts to consider what actually would light us up and why, defining aspects of that desire that are important to us, amplifying the vibration by aligning our energy with the frequency of what we're asking for.

This desire might not show up within that particular month and that's ok. Focus is key, as too is letting go to prepare for the next desire.

The questions and prompts may be answered by writing these in the spaces provided without worrying about revising, or in the form of an exercise with a friend or within your Spark Circle who fully support you.

DAY ONE - MAKE A CHOICE

Select a Singular Desire You'd Love to Manifest

WEEK ONE - GET CLEAR

Get Clear on Your Desire's Specific Aspects

WEEK TWO - REALLY FEEL IT

Become a Vibration Match by Feeling the Corresponding Emotions

WEEK THREE - ACT AS IF

Magnify the Vibration of Your Desire by Embodying It in Your Life

WEEK FOUR - LET IT GO

Let Go of Your Attachment and Move Forward in Peace

1

Start by brainstorming ideas of what you'd love to be, do or have.
Have fun with this and allow yourself to consider what would
light you up!

2

Define the aspects of this desire that important to you.
Allow yourself to consider, without limitation, what does this desire
look like and how does it feel.

3

You've identified your singular focus, what it looks like and what it
feels like. Now it's time to feel those emotions of having already
received your desire now, to the best of your ability, regardless.

4

Continue to practise visualising and feeling your desire, and magnify
it by acting as if this is who you already are! We're building upon the
feelings of having already received our desire, to acting as if it's
already in our lives.

5

Let go of the need to know how it will all come about; allowing you
to move forward in peace. Letting go creates space. And it's this space
that all the magic can fit in and express itself. Allow your desire to be
revealed in the exciting ways that they will!

MAKE A CHOICE

Select a Singular Desire You'd Love to Manifest

~

'The entire universe is conspiring
to give you everything you want."
–Abraham Hicks

Here you get to choose one desire you'd love to manifest.
You can start by brainstorming ideas of what you'd love to be, do or
have. Have fun with this and allow yourself to consider what would
light you up!

What singular desire would I love to manifest?

Sometimes we know exactly what we want!
Start by brainstorming ideas of what you'd love to be, do or have.

....

....

....

....

....

....

....

....

....

....

....

....

....

....

....

....

....

....

....

....

....

What would be a game changer?

*Could it be an experience, a lifestyle change, an item you've always
wanted, or simply a state of being and feeling.*

....

....

....

....

....

....

....

....

....

What have I been wanting... but denying?

*Sometimes we do know what we want... but we deny it, push it down, because
we don't know how to get it, don't feel worthy of it, or just don't want to get
excited only to be disappointed if it doesn't come about.*

....

....

....

....

....

....

....

....

....

Sometimes, we honestly don't know what we want.

Maybe our needs haven't been first in line for a long time, or because we haven't given ourselves the chance to consider what we even want, or we just haven't imagined anything other then our current reality, and we're out of inspiration. If you're not sure about what you want, it's helpful to first define what you don't want.

What don't I want?

....

....

....

....

....

....

....

....

....

....

....

....

....

....

....

....

Next to each item you no longer want to experience, write the opposite.

What do I want instead?

What do I need more of in my life?

What do I need less of in my life?

What do I feel influenced to go after right now?

....

....

....

....

....

....

....

....

....

....

Do I actually want to pursue any of these, or are they someone else's
expectation of what I should want?

....

....

....

....

....

....

....

....

....

....

"So many of us choose our path out of fear disguised as practicality.
What we really want seems impossibly out of reach and ridiculous to
expect so we never dare ask the universe for it.
I'm saying that I'm proof that you can ask the universe for it."
-Jim Carrey

Sometimes we dance around our desires. It's like dipping our toes in
the ocean, and then an instant later, retreating.

If you don't ever really consider what you want, you have no
responsibility to go after it. And so, if it doesn't come to pass in our
lives, we can shrug it off, and think "well... I didn't really want it
anyway." And right there, we've let ourselves off the hook. But we've
equally let ourselves down, by depriving ourselves of daring to dream
of what's possible.

Treat Pinterest like a shopping catalogue for inspiration!
Save some images you're drawn too in a dedicated soulspark board. Once you've gone on a pinning spree, have a look to see if there are any similaritie.

Are there any similarities between these images?
What images are you drawn to?
Maybe the similarities are people, friends, family, connection and love.
Is there a certain vibe that you're loving? Is it certain emotions that are similar?
These similarities in the images you've pinned will likely convey desires and aspects you'd like to integrate into your life.

....

....

....

....

....

....

....

....

....

....

....

....

....

....

....

....

There's power in deciding. It's also an act of courage.

When you make a choice, you take your power back. And in that instant, you have leverage. The universal energies gather in that instant and what you've identified is now possible!

Do not underestimate the power and magic of making a choice - It's the start of everything.

In my heart, what do I really truly want to be, do or have?

....

....

....

....

....

....

....

....

....

....

....

....

....

....

....

....

....

....

....

....

....

....

Which area in my life needs the most care and attention right now?

....

....

....

....

....

....

....

....

....

....

....

....

....

....

....

....

....

....

....

....

....

....

....

All desires and ideas I've brainstormed!

List out all the ideas of that you'd love to be, do or have based on today's excises

....

....

....

....

....

....

....

....

....

....

....

....

....

....

....

....

....

....

....

....

....

....

....

Choose a singular desire from the list that you'd love to manifest?

....

....

....

....

....

....

....

....

....

....

My desire is ...

....

....

....

....

....

....

....

....

....

....

You don't need to have all the details all worked out, especially 'the how!' Your desire may start as a spark, a hint of a 'this would be nice' and you can enhance the desire by imagining the aspects that feel exciting to you. Dwelling on the spark of a desire, without it needing to be fully developed is beautiful because you truly get to co-create with the universe.

Notes

Get Clear on Your Desire's Specific Aspects

"Imagination is everything,
it is the preview of life's coming attractions."
–Albert Einstein

Define the aspects of this desire that important to you.
Allow yourself to consider, without limitation, what does this desire
look like and how does it feel.

This step is The Creation

This is the sculpturer before the clay

The artist before the canvas.

Anything is possible

Your desire made manifest is equally magical

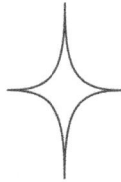

If you don't yet believe in the limitless of your creative ability,
that's ok. Use the process to guide you; cast doubt aside,
be lighthearted and go with it!

Focus on the why - Why do I want this desire?

....

....

....

....

....

....

....

....

We usually want something because we believe we will feel better having it.

How do I think I would feel if I had this desire?

....

....

....

....

....

....

....

....

....

....

....

....

....

Sometimes it can be tricky to think on the spot and describe, without limitations, exactly how you'd like a desire to be.

"Designing reality from scratch is hard. There's simply too much choice. Changing a reality that's already there is far, far easier."
-Melody Fletcher

If you could wave a wand and change your current reality
as it relates to this desire,
How would you like things to be different?

....

....

....

....

....

....

....

....

....

....

....

....

....

....

....

....

....

....

What aspects of this desire are important to me?

(even if I have no idea how these could come about)

....

....

....

....

....

....

....

....

....

What am I not willing to give up in order to receive this desire?

These are your terms!

....

....

....

....

....

....

....

....

....

....

You don't have to include elements that are deflating in your vision.
Define what you prefer and a way will be made,
and you'll be inspired to it.

There are no limitations. You get to design it your way. Please don't
dilute your desires and the aspects that are important to you!

"I'm in love with how your soul's a mix of chaos and art, and how you
never try to keep them apart." -Dermot Kennedy

The more honest and true to yourself you are, the deeper you dare to
dream, the brighter the manifestation will be as it reveals itself to you.

I like the idea of this desire overall

I like these aspects:

- ....
- ....
- ....
- ....
- ....
- ....
- ....

I don't like these aspects:

- ....
- ....
- ....
- ....
- ....
- ....
- ....
- ....

Have a clear picture of what this desire looks like

You've set your intention, and the mind focuses. In this step, we are essentially putting the mind to work for us!

There's a part of the brain called the reticular activating system. It's the part of the brain that is responsible for taking all the stimulus in our world and highlighting what's important to us, to make sure that we see it!

And you tell your mind what's important by what you focus on.

What does this desire look like?

Have a clear picture. If I were describing a photo of this desire, what would it look like? Don't limit yourself here, get excited, let your imagination run wild!

....

....

....

....

....

....

....

....

....

....

....

....

....

....

....

....

....

....

....

....

....

....

....

Remember, your choice of words are important in evoking the desired feeling and frequency

My desire,   looks like:

....

....

- ....

- ....

- ....

- ....

- ....

- ....

My desire,   feels like:

- ....

- ....

- ....

- ....

- ....

- ....

- ....

- ....

- ....

- ....

My desire,

looks like

and feels like

Notes

Exercise

TAKE IT FURTHER BY CREATING A VISION BOARD

You might like to create vision board for your desire!
Here are some ideas:

Create a physical vision board for your desire, using a pin board
or decorative frame and hang it in your space.

Get creative and use the next few pages as a place to draw, scrapbook
or collage aspects of your desire.

Create a digital vision board and save the image as your laptop
and/or phone wallpaper. Visit soulsparkjournal.com/vision-board
to download our digital vision board resources.

If you're feeling really savvy, you could even create a moving image
video vision board and overlay a favourite song that enhances the
visuals.

Notes

Become a Vibration Match by Feeling the Corresponding Emotions

~

"What you think you become. What you feel you attract.
What you imagine you create."
–Buddha

You've identified your singular focus, what it looks like and what it
feels like. Now it's time to feel those emotions now,
to the best of your ability, regardless!

Why do I want this desire? What would this mean to me?
Amp-up the heart-felt emotion of this desire. Ask yourself why do you want the desire until you get to a really good feeing.

....

....

....

....

....

....

....

....

....

....

....

....

....

....

....

....

....

....

....

....

....

....

How does my inner guidance feel about this desire?

In order to receive our desires, we need to be a vibrational match by feeling the emotions of having already received what we're asking for.

We've all probably heard this before, and it's one of the most... let's say, ~~frustrating~~ ironic aspects of intentionally applying the law of attraction. Because we're all thinking:
'We'll if I had my desire, I would feel like I have it wouldn't I!'

If you think "I want the house, I want the house, I want the house — but I *don't have* the house!" - You'll keep getting 'I want it and *I don't have it*' because that's the *feeling*.

Regardless of how we feel about the laws of the universe, it's not very productive to debate it or get frustrated by it. In fact, it feels pretty powerless to do so.

It's much more effective to find a way instead to just *be* that vibrational match.

After all, we want what we want because we believe we'll feel better having it. And we can feel those feelings now, regardless!

In feeling those heart-felt emotions now, we ensure we bypass the spiral of doubt and frustration — hooking into the absence of the desire.

> "The most powerful thing you can do—the thing that will give you much greater leverage than any action—is to spend time every day visualizing your life as you want it to be."
> -Abraham Hicks

It's natural for the mind to start plotting a plan from where you stand, but try your best to disregard that impulse! Go straight to the end result: visualize, dream it, and explore that feeling of yourself already in your desire.

It takes the strength to cast aside doubt, and reaffirm the faith by daring to feel first!

Intention + Heartfelt Emotion

On the following page is the visualisation ritual I felt inspired to craft to deliberately and most effectively place ourselves in a vibrational place of receiving all that we're asking for.

You're welcome to listen to the audio format by downloading it from soulsparkjournal.com/vhv-audio

Practise the Vibrational Harmony Visualisation daily during this week, for as long as it feels good for you!

And if you're interested in diving in deeper, here's how it works...

First, connecting with your heart decreases stress and anxiety and signals that your body is safe. When your heart beats in synchrony with the energy of appreciation, it harmonises the heart and mind into to a cohesive rhythm.

Visualising yourself in your desire is a powerful way to create a feeling of what you want. As you focus, you activate the frequency of what that desire or object represents to you and you feel that corresponding emotion.

When you activate a feeling, you can literally feel the energetic momentum. The exciting part is that the first manifestation you'll receive is the *feeling.*

Feeling those emotions of your ideal outcome, to the best of your ability helps you to ease any discomfort of how it all might be received - separating your thoughts from the past, and away from others experiences, towards your new reality.

All infinite possibilities exist in the quantum field. When we allow ourselves to be immersed into this visualisation, we're collapsing those possibilities of a wave, into a particle - using the power of our intention plus heartfelt emotion to create our new reality!

Practise the Vibrational Harmony Visualisation daily during this week, for as long as it feels good for you!

"Everything is energy and that's all there is to it. Match the frequency of the reality you want and you cannot help but get that reality. It can be no other way. This is not philosophy. This is physics."
–Albert Einstein

Vibrational Harmony Visualisation

It can be uncomfortable for our mind to go places that are unfamiliar, so you might like to start with a disclaimer to your mind —
"I'm trying something new and it's probably going to feel a little odd and strange because it's unfamiliar. But, I'm choosing to do this and I ask my mind to go along with this experiment and adventure. Please suspend all doubt and disbelief for a month and let's just see what happens!"

1   Connect to Your Heart

Shift your focus to the area of your heart, and slowly inhale and exhale. After a few breaths, feel the feeling of appreciation for anything or anyone, to the best of your ability.

2   Think of Your Clear Specific Desire

Focus on this for a few seconds ... 17 seconds

3   Visualise Yourself in the Desire

See, hear, taste, touch and feel with your imagination yourself in the desire.

4   Feel the Feeling of an Ideal Outcome

Even if you have no idea how it came about!

5   Feel the Emotions to Their Maximum Effect

Feel it all now regardless. Feel so appreciative for it being received by you.

Enjoying the feeling, then off to enjoy your day and follow what feels fun!

Notes

Q&A

How often would you recommend practicing the visualisation?
Once everyday during week two and three, for as long as it feels good - whether that's a minute or five minutes.

I'm getting pulled out of the moment by reading, do you have an audio of the visualisation I can listen to?
Yes! The audio format of the vibrational harmony visualisation is available to download from soulsparkjournal.com/vhv-audio

What if my visualisation doesn't feel good, but feels negative?
If it feels negative, you're activating the absence of the desire. This could simply be in the visualisation, you're thinking you really want this, but you don't know how to make it yours. Maybe you're feeling the fear of never having this, jealousy for others who have it or doubt it could ever be yours. These feelings are all very common, and simply mean the visualisation is activating the absence of the desire - It's just a signal you're pointed in the wrong direction!

As you focus, you activate the frequency of what that desire or object represents to you and you feel a corresponding emotion. Then as you keep focusing and feeling, the law of attraction will bring to you thoughts and memories that match that same frequency.

So if an aspect of your visualisation feel negative, ditch focusing on that aspect! Pivot and select a different aspect.

Does it feel positive? Awesome! What is that specific emotion?
What are aspects of this desire that feel good to focus on?
Keep that feeling focused in the front of mind. Keep it simple and feel it to the best of your ability.

If, as you practise the visualisation, your mind starts
highlighting why this couldn't possibly come about or be true for you; you
might like to complete the following exercise 'disputing a belief'

It can seem easier to push these thoughts aside in the moment and try and
ignore them, but they may fester in the background. After all, the law of attraction
brings to us predominantly what we're feeling, not just what we're thinking. It can be
very effective to address these and use your mind productively to disprove these
doubtful thoughts!

Why couldn't this possibly come about for me?

....

....

....

....

....

Try to restate this into a concise sentence starting with 'I'

(e.g. I can have love or money but not both)

....

....

Can I recognise that this 'point of view' is based on a limited set of data?

....

....

....

....

Can I collect facts from other people that disputes this?

....

....

....

....

Can I collect facts from other sources that dispute this?

....

....

....

....

....

Turn the statement around

(e.g. I can have love and money)

....

....

Which perspective would I like to adopt going forward?

(e.g. love and money is available to me and my partner)

....

....

....

....

Notes

Notes

Thoughts on Resistance

*"You don't have to go back and clean up that resistance,
you just can't look at it without it being a blockade."*
-Abraham Hicks

I believe focusing on 'blocks' is counterproductive. I don't want to make resistance something bigger than it needs to be.

If there's a subject that is bothering you, that when you look at it you notice you have a strong emotional reaction; try and drop that subject for a little while. Working yourself into a tizzy thinking you must be blocked is not a good feeling. Let's just let it all go that we're blocked or screwed up and therefore our dreams can't manifest. I don't believe that that's at all true.

Maybe resistance is a natural sorting of an aspect you don't really want. Maybe it's best not to 'release' a resistant thought or belief but be more discerning in selecting aspects of our intentions.

I like the idea of this desire overall

I like these aspects:

-
-
-

I don't like these aspects:

-
-
-

What am I feeling not-so-good about?

How would I like to feel?

How can I move towards this?

ACT AS IF

Magnify the Vibration of Your Desire by Embodying It in Your Life

⌒

"The Universe does not distinguish between your thoughts
of current reality and thoughts of imagined reality.
The Universe and the Law of Attraction are simply
responding to your thoughts—
real or imagined, current or remembered."
–Abraham Hicks

Continue to practise visualising and feeling your desire,
and magnify it by acting as if this is who you already are!
We're building upon the feelings of having already received
our desire, to acting as if it's already in our lives.

It can seem like you are the one that will need to make this desire come about, through hard work and action, but this can actually be a sign you're pointed in the wrong direction. Because in doing so, you may be activating the 'absence of the desire' and therefore perpetuating a state of not-having-it.

It's much more effective to address any misaligned feelings and bring them to our awareness. That way, we can intentionally steer ourselves in a vibrational place of receiving all that we are asking for.

How would I imagine someone who has this desire...
If you're not sure, just imagine and make it up!
...thinks and feels about this?

....

....

....

....

....

....

... speaks to themselves and speaks to others about this?

....

....

....

....

....

....

... carries themselves?

....

....

....

....

....

... goes about their day?

....

....

....

....

....

....

....

How is this different from how I currently think, speak and act?

....

....

....

....

....

....

....

....

....

....

....

....

....

Vibrational Harmony Visualisation

Practise the Vibrational Harmony Visualisation daily during this week,
for as long as it feels good for you!
You're welcome to listen to the audio format by downloading it from
soulsparkjournal.com/vhv-audio

1   Connect to your heart

*Shift your focus to the area of your heart, and slowly inhale and exhale.
After a few breaths, feel the feeling of appreciation for anything or anyone,
to the best of your ability.*

2   Think of your clear specific desire

Focus on this for a few seconds ... 17 seconds

3   Visualise yourself in the desire.

See, hear, taste, touch and feel with your imagination yourself in the desire.

4   Feel the feeling of an ideal outcome

Even if you have no idea how it came about!

5   Feel it to the best of your ability, to the maximum effect!

Feel it all now regardless. Feel so appreciative for it being received by you.

Enjoying the feeling then off to enjoy your day and follow what feels fun!

Just as we know the level of the problem is not at the level of the solution; the level of a desire is not at the level of receiving it.

Through my own experiences, the conclusion I came to about vibrational harmony was with a simplified analogy: If I already have something, (say a handbag) I feel like I have it - because I do, I own it.

The feeling of actually owning something is quite different from experiencing an ongoing awareness that something isn't mine and that I didn't have it.

I invite you to think about an item you once wanted that you now own. How does it feel to you now? I bet it feels like it's yours, you own it. You may like it or you might feel indifferent about it now, but regardless, you have an expectation that you own it and that it's yours.

If I imagine someone who already has this desire,

Is there something they consistently do to maintain having this in their lives?

...everyday

....

....

....

....

....

....

... every week

....

....

....

....

....

....

... every month

....

....

....

....

....

If this desire was already in my life, what things would I do
differently?

....

....

....

....

....

....

....

....

....

....

....

....

....

....

....

....

....

....

....

....

....

Vibrational harmony is feeling like you already have the desire you want. It's that subtle shift in appreciating it *and* feeling as though it's already yours!

"Total believer, yeah I believe in manifestation. I believe in putting a rocket of desire out into the universe. And you get it when you believe it, when you believe you have it and that's the key.

People sit around going:

'When's it gonna come?'

'When's it gonna come?'

'When's it gonna come?'

'When's it gonna come?'

And that's the wrong way.

You're facing the wrong way, you're facing away from it.

You have to go 'it's here, it's here, it's here' "

-Jim Carrey, speaking to Oprah about how he manifested 10 million dollars from nothing.

Imagine you are an actor and you're going to embody the best version of yourself and that your desire is a done deal!

How would I act?

....

....

....

....

....

....

....

....

What would my day be like?

....

....

....

....

....

....

....

....

....

....

Imagine you are an actor and you're going to embody the best version of yourself and that your desire is a done deal!

How is my body language?

....
....
....
....
....
....
....
....

How is my tone?

....
....
....
....
....
....
....
....
....
....

Which of these characteristics could I choose to fully embrace?

....

....

....

....

....

....

....

....

....

....

....

....

....

....

....

....

....

....

....

....

....

Do I have concerns about embracing these parts of myself?

....

....

....

....

....

....

....

....

....

....

....

....

....

....

....

....

....

....

....

....

....

....

....

....

How does my inner guidance feel about these concerns?

....

....

....

....

....

....

....

....

....

....

....

....

....

....

....

....

....

....

....

....

....

....

....

What could I start incorporating that will empower me to
move forward?

....

....

....

....

....

....

....

....

....

....

....

....

....

....

....

....

....

....

....

....

From this place of acting as if my desire is a done-deal,
what am I excited to do?

....

....

....

....

....

....

....

....

....

....

....

....

....

....

....

....

....

....

Practise those in your days!

Notes

....

....

....

....

....

....

....

....

....

....

....

....

....

....

....

....

....

....

....

....

....

As you follow the guided process to manifest your desires, if your mind starts highlighting why this couldn't possibly come about or be true for you; you might like to complete this disputing a thought pattern exercise.

It can seem easier to push these thoughts aside in the moment and try and ignore them, but they may fester in the background. After all, the law of attraction brings to us predominantly what we're feeling, not just what we're thinking. I believe it's more effective to address these head on and use our mind

Why couldn't this possibly come about for me?

....

....

....

....

....

Try to restate this into a concise sentence starting with 'I'

(e.g. I can have love or money but not both)

....

....

Can I recognise that this 'point of view' is based on a limited set of data?

....

....

....

....

Can I collect facts from other people that disputes this?

....

....

....

....

Can I collect facts from other sources that dispute this?

....

....

....

....

....

Turn the statement around

(e.g. I can have love and money)

....

....

Which perspective would I like to adopt going forward?

(e.g. love and money is available to me and my partner)

....

....

....

....

Let Go of Your Attachment and Move Forward in Peace

"So many times people who do that process live in the
space of wanting and resisting it. instead of writing it,
visualising it, seeing it for yourself and then letting it go.
Letting it go but moving in the direction
of working towards it."
–Oprah Winfrey

Let go of the need to know how it will all come about; allowing you
to move forward in peace. Letting go creates space. And it's this space
that all the magic can fit in and express itself. Allow your desire to be
revealed in the exciting ways that they will!

Am I using action to compensate for misaligned feelings and
energy?

....

....

....

....

....

....

....

....

....

....

What am I doing to make this desire come about?
Through my action, time and energy

....

....

....

....

....

....

....

....

....

How does it feel when I take these actions?

Is it uplifting and fun? Or does it feel like a burden and deflating...

....

....

....

....

....

....

....

....

....

....

....

....

....

....

....

....

....

....

....

....

....

....

I've come to appreciate that the energetic vibration of holding a desire tightly, heart-set on making it manifest, is a sure-fire way to ensure... we never receive it.

This could express itself in feelings of resentment, jealousy, defensiveness, blame; any of those constricting states that disallow what-is. Or, wishing for a different outcome in the past and being hung up on it, usually to our detriment.

Not letting go of a desire means we're holding onto a reality so tightly that there is no room for the possibility of something new to come in ways we weren't expecting, perhaps something more enjoyable, or something more aligned for our highest good.

At some point, we just have to let things go.
We have to trust that we have done all that we can do
to intentionally receive our desire.

So for the final week in this process, I invite you to practise letting go
of the need to know how your desire will come about.
It takes tremendous courage to trust, but trust is what is needed now.

Letting Go

Practice letting go and moving forward in peace
by reading this script to yourself daily during this week.

"

From this day-
I commit to stop analysing why things perhaps haven't gone better as
they relate to this desire, and instead, I choose to let go and let them be
better!

I allow all to be revealed, and I'm excited in the ways that they will!
And in doing so, I give myself permission to feel good now, to feel
how I want to feel regardless of when or how this comes into my life.

I choose to let go of trying to control the 'how' how it will all come
about, and I'm choosing to let go of my attachment to this desire.

I'm deciding to no longer compensate for misaligned energy by offering
more time or action. Just like a helpful assistant taking care of all of the
details in the background, I trust that my desire is coming to me all in
perfect timing, and I trust that if something is required of me, I will feel
the intuitive nudge that will bring it to my attention.

I choose to move forward in a state of peace, taking action when it feels
great to do so from a place of intention.

I let go of my need to know how it will all come about. I know that
letting go creates space. And it's this space that all of the magic can flow
in and express itself. I gently flow with life and each new experience. I
appreciate where I am, I'm so grateful, I'm excited and eager as things
unfold and get better and better!

"

Am I holding on to a reality so tightly that I'm limiting this
manifestation coming in unexpected ways?

....

....

....

....

....

....

....

....

....

....

....

....

....

....

....

....

....

....

....

....

Can I acknowledge that the universe might have something better
in store for me than I can conceive of right now?
Something more enjoyable and in alignment with my highest good

....

....

....

....

....

....

....

....

....

....

....

....

....

....

....

....

....

....

....

....

....

....

Joyously, Consciously, Create Your Own Reality

✕ Take action from a place of desire / wanting / chasing

✓ Trust in the flow of life by taking action when inspired

✕ I don't have it, therefore I'm not happy or whole.

✓ I appreciate where I am and I'm excited and eager as things unfold

Be mindful of any actions you're talking to manifest a desire that doesn't feel fun, but feels like a burden. That's a good sign that your desire and the way to get there are out of alignment and won't produce the outcome you're looking for.

Take inspired action and take advantage of opportunities when they present themselves if they come from a place of intention.

How do you know between the two?
When you have an idea or just feel like doing something, consider how you're feeling in that moment.

If you're feeling dissatisfied with the present moment: frustrated, sad, angry, or thinking about the past or the future in a longing way - any ideas you have at that moment will match up with that feeling frequency, and if followed by action, will bring more unwanted.

If you're feeling a positive state of satisfaction with the present moment, you're in alignment and should follow the flow as more good things are on the way!

How might I let go of any chronic longing, whilst still keeping the
faith that my desire will show up in divine timing?

....

....

....

....

....

....

....

....

....

....

....

....

....

....

....

....

....

....

....

....

How can I trust in the flow of life?

Letting go creates space. And it's this space that all the magic can filter in and express itself.

I love the analogy of the manager by Abraham hicks: "allowing is like standing back and trusting your manager to set things into place, trusting that when something is required of you, your manager will bring your attention to it."

Allowing yourself to feel what you want to feel and be happy now regardless. Allow it to be revealed and be exciting in the ways it will!

In the weeks and months to come, if you think back to this desire and are feeling a little ... 'I wonder when... I hope it still comes...' reaffirm by reading the letting go manifesto.

Notes

....

....

....

....

....

....

....

....

....

....

....

....

....

....

....

....

....

....

....

....

....

....

....

Notes

....

....

....

....

....

....

....

....

....

....

....

....

....

....

....

....

....

....

....

....

....

....

....

....

....

Notes

Think differently

✧

Receive guidenence

✧

Choose the right choice at the right time

✧

Change your mind

✧

Notice your true self emerging

Select a Singular Desire You'd Love to Manifest

~

"Your life changes the moment you make a new,
congruent, and committed decision."
–Tony Robbins

Here you get to choose one desire you'd love to manifest.
You can start by brainstorming ideas of what you'd love to be, do or
have. Have fun with this and allow yourself to consider what would
light you up!

What singular desire would I love to manifest?

Sometimes we know exactly what we want!
Start by brainstorming ideas of what you'd love to be, do or have.

....

....

....

....

....

....

....

....

....

....

....

....

....

....

....

....

....

....

....

....

....

....

What would be a game changer?

*Could it be an experience, a lifestyle change, an item you've always
wanted, or simply a state of being and feeling.*

....

....

....

....

....

....

....

....

....

....

What have I been wanting... but denying?

*Sometimes we do know what we want... but we deny it, push it down, because
we don't know how to get it, don't feel worthy of it, or just don't want to get
excited only to be disappointed if it doesn't come about.*

....

....

....

....

....

....

....

....

....

Sometimes, we honestly don't know what we want.

Maybe our needs haven't been first in line for a long time, or because we haven't given ourselves the chance to consider what we even want, or we just haven't imagined anything other then our current reality, and we're out of inspiration. If you're not sure about what you want, it's helpful to first define what you don't want.

What don't I want?

....

....

....

....

....

....

....

....

....

....

....

....

....

....

....

....

....

....

Next to each item you no longer want to experience, write the opposite.

What do I want instead?

....

....

....

....

....

....

....

....

....

....

....

....

....

....

....

....

....

....

....

....

....

....

What do I need more of in my life?

....

....

....

....

....

....

....

....

....

What do I need less of in my life?

....

....

....

....

....

....

....

....

....

....

What do I feel influenced to go after right now?

....

....

....

....

....

....

....

....

....

....

Do I actually want to pursue any of these, or are they someone else's
expectation of what I should want?

....

....

....

....

....

....

....

....

....

....

....

Treat Pinterest like a shopping catalogue for inspiration!
Save some images you're drawn too in a dedicated soulspark board. Once you've gone on a pinning spree, have a look to see if there are any similaritie.

Are there any similarities between these images?
What images are you drawn to?
Maybe the similarities are people, friends, family, connection and love.
Is there a certain vibe that you're loving? Is it certain emotions that are similar?
These similarities in the images you've pinned will likely convey desires and aspects you'd like to integrate into your life.

....

....

....

....

....

....

....

....

....

....

....

....

....

....

....

....

In my heart, what do I really truly want to be, do or have?

Which area in my life needs the most care and attention right now?

....

....

....

....

....

....

....

....

....

....

....

....

....

....

....

....

....

....

....

....

....

....

....

....

....

All desires and ideas I've brainstormed!

List out all the ideas of that you'd love to be, do or have based on today's excises

....
....
....
....
....
....
....
....
....
....
....
....
....
....
....
....
....
....
....
....
....

Choose a singular desire from the list that you'd love to manifest?

....

....

....

....

....

....

....

....

....

....

My desire is ...

....

....

....

....

....

....

....

....

....

....

Notes

Get Clear on Your Desire's Specific Aspects

~

"You are the designer of your destiny;
you are the author of your story."
–Lisa Nichols

Define the aspects of this desire that important to you. Allow yourself
to consider, without limitation, what does this desire look like and
how does it feel.

Focus on the why - Why do I want this desire?

....

....

....

....

....

....

....

....

We usually want something because we believe we will feel better having it.

How do I think I would feel if I had this desire?

....

....

....

....

....

....

....

....

....

....

....

....

If you could wave a wand and change your current reality
as it relates to this desire,
How would you like things to be different?

....

....

....

....

....

....

....

....

....

....

....

....

....

....

....

....

....

....

....

....

What aspects of this desire are important to me?

(even if I have no idea how these could come about)

....

....

....

....

....

....

....

....

What am I not willing to give up in order to receive this desire?

These are your terms!

....

....

....

....

....

....

....

....

....

....

....

I like the idea of this desire overall

I like these aspects:

- ....
- ....
- ....
- ....
- ....
- ....
- ....
- ....

I don't like these aspects:

- ....
- ....
- ....
- ....
- ....
- ....
- ....
- ....
- ....

What does this desire look like?

Have a clear picture. If I were describing a photo of this desire, what would it look like? Don't limit yourself here, get excited, let your imagination run wild!

....

....

....

....

....

....

....

....

....

....

....

....

....

....

....

....

....

....

....

....

....

....

Remember, your choice of words are important in evoking the desired feeling and frequency

My desire,   looks like:

....

....

  •
....

  •
....

  •
....

  •
....

  •
....

  •
....

My desire,   feels like:

....

  •
....

  •
....

  •
....

  •
....

  •
....

  •
....

  •
....

  •
....

My desire,

looks like

and feels like

Notes

Exercise

TAKE IT FURTHER BY CREATING A VISION BOARD

You might like to create vision board for your desire!
Here are some ideas:

Create a physical vision board for your desire, using a pin board
or decorative frame and hang it in your space.

Get creative and use the next few pages as a place to draw, scrapbook
or collage aspects of your desire.

Create a digital vision board and save the image as your laptop
and/or phone wallpaper. Visit soulsparkjournal.com/vision-board
to download our digital vision board resources.

If you're feeling really savvy, you could even create a moving image
video vision board and overlay a favourite song that enhances the
visuals.

Notes

....

....

....

....

....

....

....

....

....

....

....

....

....

....

....

....

....

....

....

....

....

Become a Vibration Match by Feeling the Corresponding Emotions

~

"Any given moment contains unlimited futures that can
become real. The reality that occurs is the one
you pay attention to."
–Penny Peirce

You've identified your singular focus, what it looks like and what it
feels like. Now it's time to feel those emotions now,
to the best of your ability, regardless!

Why do I want this desire? What would this mean to me?
*Amp-up the heart-felt emotion of this desire. Ask yourself why do you want the
desire until you get to a really good feeing.*

....

....

....

....

....

....

....

....

....

....

....

....

....

....

....

....

....

....

....

....

....

....

....

How does my inner guidance feel about this desire?

....

....

....

....

....

....

....

....

....

....

....

....

....

....

....

....

....

....

....

....

....

Intention + Heartfelt Emotion

On the following page is the visualisation ritual I felt inspired to craft to deliberately and most effectively place ourselves in a vibrational place of receiving all that we're asking for.

You're welcome to listen to the audio format by downloading it from soulsparkjournal.com/vhv-audio

Practise the Vibrational Harmony Visualisation daily during this week, for as long as it feels good for you!

And if you're interested in diving in deeper, here's how it works...

First, connecting with your heart decreases stress and anxiety and signals that your body is safe. When your heart beats in synchrony with the energy of appreciation, it harmonises the heart and mind into to a cohesive rhythm.

Visualising yourself in your desire is a powerful way to create a feeling of what you want. As you focus, you activate the frequency of what that desire or object represents to you and you feel that corresponding emotion.

When you activate a feeling, you can literally feel the energetic momentum. The exciting part is that the first manifestation you'll receive is the *feeling*

Feeling those emotions of your ideal outcome, to the best of your ability helps you to ease any discomfort of how it all might be received - separating your thoughts from the past, and away from others experiences. towards your new reality.

All infinite possibilities exist in the quantum field. When we allow ourselves to be immersed into this visualisation, we're collapsing those possibilities of a wave, into a particle - using the power of our intention plus heartfelt emotion to create our new reality!

Practise the Vibrational Harmony Visualisation daily during this week, for as long as it feels good for you!

"Everything is energy and that's all there is to it. Match the frequency of the reality you want and you cannot help but get that reality. It can be no other way. This is not philosophy. This is physics."
–Albert Einstein

Vibrational Harmony Visualisation

It can be uncomfortable for our mind to go places that are unfamiliar, so you might like to start with a disclaimer to your mind —

"I'm trying something new and it's probably going to feel a little odd and strange because it's unfamiliar. But, I'm choosing to do this and I ask my mind to go along with this experiment and adventure. Please suspend all doubt and disbelief for a month and let's just see what happens!"

1   Connect to Your Heart

Shift your focus to the area of your heart, and slowly inhale and exhale. After a few breaths, feel the feeling of appreciation for anything or anyone, to the best of your ability.

2   Think of Your Clear Specific Desire

Focus on this for a few seconds ... 17 seconds

3   Visualise Yourself in the Desire

See, hear, taste, touch and feel with your imagination yourself in the desire.

4   Feel the Feeling of an Ideal Outcome

Even if you have no idea how it came about!

5   Feel the Emotions to Their Maximum Effect

Feel it all now regardless. Feel so appreciative for it being received by you.

Enjoying the feeling, then off to enjoy your day and follow what feels fun!

Notes

....

....

....

....

....

....

....

....

....

....

....

....

....

....

....

....

....

....

....

....

....

....

....

....

....

Q&A

How often would you recommend practicing the visualisation?
Once everyday during week two and three, for as long as it feels good - whether that's a minute or five minutes.

I'm getting pulled out of the moment by reading, do you have an audio of the visualisation I can listen to?
Yes! The audio format of the vibrational harmony visualisation is available to download from soulsparkjournal.com/vhv-audio

What if my visualisation doesn't feel good, but feels negative?
If it feels negative, you're activating the absence of the desire. This could simply be in the visualisation, you're thinking you really want this, but you don't know how to make it yours. Maybe you're feeling the fear of never having this, jealousy for others who have it or doubt it could ever be yours. These feelings are all very common, and simply mean the visualisation is activating the absence of the desire - It's just a signal you're pointed in the wrong direction!

As you focus, you activate the frequency of what that desire or object represents to you and you feel a corresponding emotion. Then as you keep focusing and feeling, the law of attraction will bring to you thoughts and memories that match that same frequency.

So if an aspect of your visualisation feel negative, ditch focusing on that aspect! Pivot and select a different aspect.

Does it feel positive? Awesome! What is that specific emotion? What are aspects of this desire that feel good to focus on? Keep that feeling focused in the front of mind. Keep it simple and feel it to the best of your ability.

If, as you practise the visualisation, your mind starts
highlighting why this couldn't possibly come about or be true for you; you
might like to complete the following exercise 'disputing a belief'

It can seem easier to push these thoughts aside in the moment and try and
ignore them, but they may fester in the background. After all, the law of attraction
brings to us predominantly what we're feeling, not just what we're thinking. It can be
very effective to address these and use your mind productively to disprove these
doubtful thoughts!

Why couldn't this possibly come about for me?

....

....

....

....

....

Try to restate this into a concise sentence starting with 'I'

(e.g. I can have love _or_ money but not both)

....

....

Can I recognise that this 'point of view' is based on a limited set of data?

....

....

....

....

Can I collect facts from other people that disputes this?

....

....

....

....

Can I collect facts from other sources that dispute this?

....

....

....

....

....

Turn the statement around

(e.g. I can have love _and_ money)

....

....

Which perspective would I like to adopt going forward?

(e.g. love and money is available to me and my partner)

....

....

....

....

Notes

Notes

ENERGY CHECK IN

What am I feeling not-so-good about?

How would I like to feel?

How can I move towards this?

ACT AS IF

Magnify the Vibration of Your Desire by Embodying It in Your Life

~

"When you devote your life to the things that fill you up,
the universe can't help but support you.
You don't need to know how, just trust that it will."
–Rebecca Campbell

Continue to practise visualising and feeling your desire,
and magnify it by acting as if this is who you already are!
We're building upon the feelings of having already received
our desire, to acting as if it's already in our lives.

How would I imagine someone who has this desire...
If you're not sure, just imagine and make it up!
...thinks and feels about this?

....

....

....

....

....

....

... speaks to themselves and speaks to others about this?

....

....

....

....

....

....

... carries themselves?

....

....

....

....

....

....

... goes about their day?

....

....

....

....

....

....

....

How is this different from how I currently think, speak and act?

....

....

....

....

....

....

....

....

....

....

....

....

....

....

....

Vibrational Harmony Visualisation

Practise the Vibrational Harmony Visualisation daily during this week,
for as long as it feels good for you!
You're welcome to listen to the audio format by downloading it from
soulsparkjournal.com/vhv-audio

1   Connect to your heart

*Shift your focus to the area of your heart, and slowly inhale and exhale.
After a few breaths, feel the feeling of appreciation for anything or anyone,
to the best of your ability.*

2   Think of your clear specific desire

Focus on this for a few seconds ... 17 seconds

3   Visualise yourself in the desire.

See, hear, taste, touch and feel with your imagination yourself in the desire.

4   Feel the feeling of an ideal outcome

Even if you have no idea how it came about!

5   Feel it to the best of your ability, to the maximum effect!

Feel it all now regardless. Feel so appreciative for it being received by you.

Enjoying the feeling, then off to enjoy your day and follow what feels fun!

If I imagine someone who already has this desire,

Is there something they consistently do to maintain having this in their lives?

...everyday

....

....

....

....

....

....

... every week

....

....

....

....

....

... every month

....

....

....

....

....

If this desire was already in my life, what things would I do
differently?

....

....

....

....

....

....

....

....

....

....

....

....

....

....

....

....

....

....

....

....

....

....

Imagine you are an actor and you're going to embody the best version of yourself and that your desire is a done deal!

How would I act?

....

....

....

....

....

....

....

....

....

What would my day be like?

....

....

....

....

....

....

....

....

....

....

Imagine you are an actor and you're going to embody the best version of yourself and that your desire is a done deal!

How is my body language?

....
....
....
....
....
....
....
....
....

How is my tone?

....
....
....
....
....
....
....
....
....
....
....

Which of these characteristics could I choose to fully embrace?

....

....

....

....

....

....

....

....

....

....

....

....

....

....

....

....

....

....

....

....

....

....

....

....

Do I have concerns about embracing these parts of myself?

How does my inner guidance feel about these concerns?

....

....

....

....

....

....

....

....

....

....

....

....

....

....

....

....

....

....

....

....

....

What could I start incorporating that will empower me to
move forward?

....

....

....

....

....

....

....

....

....

....

....

....

....

....

....

....

....

....

....

....

....

....

....

From this place of acting as if my desire is a done-deal,
what am I excited to do?

....
....
....
....
....
....
....
....
....
....
....
....
....
....
....
....
....
....
....
....
....

Practise those in your days!

Notes

As you follow the guided process to manifest your desires, if your mind starts highlighting why this couldn't possibly come about or be true for you; you might like to complete this disputing a thought pattern exercise.

It can seem easier to push these thoughts aside in the moment and try and ignore them, but they may fester in the background. After all, the law of attraction brings to us predominantly what we're feeling, not just what we're thinking. I believe it's more effective to address these head on and use our mind

Why couldn't this possibly come about for me?

....

....

....

....

....

Try to restate this into a concise sentence starting with 'I'

(e.g. I can have love _or_ money but not both)

....

....

Can I recognise that this 'point of view' is based on a limited set of data?

....

....

....

....

Can I collect facts from other people that disputes this?

....

....

....

....

Can I collect facts from other sources that dispute this?

....

....

....

....

....

Turn the statement around

(e.g. I can have love and money)

....

....

Which perspective would I like to adopt going forward?

(e.g. love and money is available to me and my partner)

....

....

....

....

Let Go of Your Attachment and Move Forward in Peace

"Trust yourself and the divine in you. Know that all things
are working together to support you living your best life."
–Lisa Nichols

Let go of the need to know how it will all come about; allowing you
to move forward in peace. Letting go creates space. And it's this space
that all the magic can fit in and express itself. Allow your desire to be
revealed in the exciting ways that they will!

Am I using action to compensate for misaligned feelings and
energy?

....

....

....

....

....

....

....

....

....

....

What am I doing to make this desire come about?
Through my action, time and energy

....

....

....

....

....

....

....

....

....

How does it feel when I take these actions?

Is it uplifting and fun? Or does it feel like a burden and deflating...

....

....

....

....

....

....

....

....

....

....

....

....

....

....

....

....

....

....

....

....

....

....

....

Letting Go

Practice letting go and moving forward in peace
by reading this script to yourself daily during this week.

66

From this day-
I commit to stop analysing why things perhaps haven't gone better as
they relate to this desire, and instead, I choose to let go and let them be
better!

I allow all to be revealed, and I'm excited in the ways that they will!
And in doing so, I give myself permission to feel good now, to feel
how I want to feel regardless of when or how this comes into my life.

I choose to let go of trying to control the 'how' how it will all come
about, and I'm choosing to let go of my attachment to this desire.

I'm deciding to no longer compensate for misaligned energy by offering
more time or action. Just like a helpful assistant taking care of all of the
details in the background, I trust that my desire is coming to me all in
perfect timing, and I trust that if something is required of me, I will feel
the intuitive nudge that will bring it to my attention.

I choose to move forward in a state of peace, taking action when it feels
great to do so from a place of intention.

I let go of my need to know how it will all come about. I know that
letting go creates space. And it's this space that all of the magic can flow
in and express itself. I gently flow with life and each new experience. I
appreciate where I am, I'm so grateful, I'm excited and eager as things
unfold and get better and better!

99

Am I holding on to a reality so tightly that I'm limiting this
manifestation coming in unexpected ways?

....

....

....

....

....

....

....

....

....

....

....

....

....

....

....

....

....

....

....

....

....

Can I acknowledge that the universe might have something better
in store for me than I can conceive of right now?

Something more enjoyable and in alignment with my highest good

....

....

....

....

....

....

....

....

....

....

....

....

....

....

....

....

....

....

....

....

How might I let go of any chronic longing, whilst still keeping the
faith that my desire will show up in divine timing?

....
....
....
....
....
....
....
....
....
....
....
....
....
....
....
....
....
....
....
....
....
....
....

How can I trust in the flow of life?

....

....

....

....

....

....

....

....

....

....

....

....

....

....

....

....

....

....

....

....

....

....

Notes

....
....
....
....
....
....
....
....
....
....
....
....
....
....
....
....
....
....
....
....
....
....
....
....
....

Notes

....

....

....

....

....

....

....

....

....

....

....

....

....

....

....

....

....

....

....

....

....

....

....

....

Notes

Notes

I AM RELEASING

TO GAIN MORE

self-doubt

trust

excuses

perspective

shame

self-acceptance

worry

mindfulness

resentment

joy

busyness

rest

comparison

self-compassion

feelings of lack

appreciation

pain from the past

peace

negative self-talk

self-love

Select a Singular Desire You'd Love to Manifest

~

"Your present circumstances don't determine where you
can go; they merely determine where you start."
–Nido Qubein

Here you get to choose one desire you'd love to manifest.
You can start by brainstorming ideas of what you'd love to be,
do or have. Have fun with this and allow yourself to consider
what would light you up!

What singular desire would I love to manifest?

Sometimes we know exactly what we want!
Start by brainstorming ideas of what you'd love to be, do or have.

....

....

....

....

....

....

....

....

....

....

....

....

....

....

....

....

....

....

....

....

....

....

....

....

....

....

What would be a game changer?

Could it be an experience, a lifestyle change, an item you've always wanted, or simply a state of being and feeling.

....
....
....
....
....
....
....
....
....

What have I been wanting... but denying?

Sometimes we do know what we want... but we deny it, push it down, because we don't know how to get it, don't feel worthy of it, or just don't want to get excited only to be disappointed if it doesn't come about.

....
....
....
....
....
....
....
....
....

Sometimes, we honestly don't know what we want.

Maybe our needs haven't been first in line for a long time, or because we haven't given ourselves the chance to consider what we even want, or we just haven't imagined anything other then our current reality, and we're out of inspiration.

If you're not sure about what you want, it's helpful to first define what you don't want.

What don't I want?

....

....

....

....

....

....

....

....

....

....

....

....

....

....

....

....

....

....

....

....

Next to each item you no longer want to experience, write the opposite.

What do I want instead?

....

....

....

....

....

....

....

....

....

....

....

....

....

....

....

....

....

....

....

....

....

....

What do I need more of in my life?

....

....

....

....

....

....

....

....

....

What do I need less of in my life?

....

....

....

....

....

....

....

....

....

....

....

What do I feel influenced to go after right now?

....

....

....

....

....

....

....

....

....

....

Do I actually want to pursue any of these, or are they someone else's expectation of what I should want?

....

....

....

....

....

....

....

....

....

....

Treat Pinterest like a shopping catalogue for inspiration!
Save some images you're drawn too in a dedicated soulspark board. Once you've gone on a pinning spree, have a look to see if there are any similaritie.

Are there any similarities between these images?
What images are you drawn to?
Maybe the similarities are people, friends, family, connection and love.
Is there a certain vibe that you're loving? Is it certain emotions that are similar?
These similarities in the images you've pinned will likely convey desires and aspects you'd like to integrate into your life.

....
....
....
....
....
....
....
....
....
....
....
....
....
....
....
....
....

In my heart, what do I really truly want to be, do or have?

....

....

....

....

....

....

....

....

....

....

....

....

....

....

....

....

....

....

....

....

....

....

....

....

....

Which area in my life needs the most care and attention right now?

....

....

....

....

....

....

....

....

....

....

....

....

....

....

....

....

....

....

....

....

....

....

....

All desires and ideas I've brainstormed!

List out all the ideas of that you'd love to be, do or have based on today's excises

....

....

....

....

....

....

....

....

....

....

....

....

....

....

....

....

....

....

....

....

....

Choose a singular desire from the list that you'd love to manifest?

....

....

....

....

....

....

....

....

....

....

My desire is ...

....

....

....

....

....

....

....

....

....

....

Notes

Get Clear on Your Desire's Specific Aspects

~

"If you don't design your own life plan, chances are you'll
fall into someone else's plan. And guess what they have
planned for you? Not much."
–Jim Rohn

Define the aspects of this desire that important to you. Allow yourself
to consider, without limitation, what does this desire look like and
how does it feel.

Focus on the why - Why do I want this desire?

....

....

....

....

....

....

....

....

We usually want something because we believe we will feel better having it.

How do I think I would feel if I had this desire?

....

....

....

....

....

....

....

....

....

....

....

....

If you could wave a wand and change your current reality
as it relates to this desire,
How would you like things to be different?

....

....

....

....

....

....

....

....

....

....

....

....

....

....

....

....

....

....

....

....

What aspects of this desire are important to me?
(even if I have no idea how these could come about)

....

....

....

....

....

....

....

....

What am I not willing to give up in order to receive this desire?
These are your terms!

....

....

....

....

....

....

....

....

....

....

....

I like the idea of this desire overall

I like these aspects:

....
- ....
- ....
- ....
- ....
- ....
- ....
- ....

I don't like these aspects:

....
- ....
- ....
- ....
- ....
- ....
- ....
- ....
- ....
- ....

What does this desire look like?

Have a clear picture. If I were describing a photo of this desire, what would it look like? Don't limit yourself here, get excited, let your imagination run wild!

....

....

....

....

....

....

....

....

....

....

....

....

....

....

....

....

....

....

....

....

....

....

....

Remember, your choice of words are important in evoking the desired feeling and frequency

My desire, looks like:

....

....

•
....

•
....

•
....

•
....

•
....

•
....

My desire, feels like:

....

•
....

•
....

•
....

•
....

•
....

•
....

•
....

•
....

My desire,

looks like

and feels like

Notes

Exercise

TAKE IT FURTHER BY CREATING A VISION BOARD

You might like to create a vision board for your desire, such as a physical vision board; using a pin board or decorated frame.

Or you can create a digital vision board and save the image laptop or phone wallpaper!

Visit soulsparkjournal.com/vision-board to download our digital vision board resources

Notes

....

....

....

....

....

....

....

....

....

....

....

....

....

....

....

....

....

....

....

....

....

....

....

REALLY FEEL IT

Become a Vibration Match by Feeling the Corresponding Emotions

~

"Don't be afraid of your greatness, don't be afraid of how
bright and brilliant and unbelievable you are;
we don't have to dim down."
–Alicia Keys

You've identified your singular focus, what it looks like and what it
feels like. Now it's time to feel those emotions now,
to the best of your ability, regardless!

Why do I want this desire? What would this mean to me?
Amp-up the heart-felt emotion of this desire. Ask yourself why do you want the
desire until you get to a really good feeing.

....

....

....

....

....

....

....

....

....

....

....

....

....

....

....

....

....

....

....

....

....

....

....

....

How does my inner guidance feel about this desire?

....
....
....
....
....
....
....
....
....
....
....
....
....
....
....
....
....
....
....
....
....
....
....
....
....
....
....

Intention + Heartfelt Emotion

On the following page is the visualisation ritual I felt inspired to craft to deliberately and most effectively place ourselves in a vibrational place of receiving all that we're asking for.

You're welcome to listen to the audio format by downloading it from soulsparkjournal.com/vhv-audio

Practise the Vibrational Harmony Visualisation daily during this week, for as long as it feels good for you!

And if you're interested in diving in deeper, here's how it works...

First, connecting with your heart decreases stress and anxiety and signals that your body is safe. When your heart beats in synchrony with the energy of appreciation, it harmonises the heart and mind into to a cohesive rhythm.

Visualising yourself in your desire is a powerful way to create a feeling of what you want. As you focus, you activate the frequency of what that desire or object represents to you and you feel that corresponding emotion.

When you activate a feeling, you can literally feel the energetic momentum. The exciting part is that the first manifestation you'll receive is the *feeling*.

Feeling those emotions of your ideal outcome, to the best of your ability helps you to ease any discomfort of how it all might be received - separating your thoughts from the past, and away from others experiences. towards your new reality.

All infinite possibilities exist in the quantum field. When we allow ourselves to be immersed into this visualisation, we're collapsing those possibilities of a wave, into a particle - using the power of our intention plus heartfelt emotion to create our new reality!

Practise the Vibrational Harmony Visualisation daily during this week, for as long as it feels good for you!

"Everything is energy and that's all there is to it. Match the frequency of the reality you want and you cannot help but get that reality. It can be no other way. This is not philosophy. This is physics."

–Albert Einstein

Vibrational Harmony Visualisation

It can be uncomfortable for our mind to go places that are unfamiliar, so you might like to start with a disclaimer to your mind —

"I'm trying something new and it's probably going to feel a little odd and strange because it's unfamiliar. But, I'm choosing to do this and I ask my mind to go along with this experiment and adventure. Please suspend all doubt and disbelief for a month and let's just see what happens!"

1   Connect to Your Heart

Shift your focus to the area of your heart, and slowly inhale and exhale. After a few breaths, feel the feeling of appreciation for anything or anyone, to the best of your ability.

2   Think of Your Clear Specific Desire

Focus on this for a few seconds ... 17 seconds

3   Visualise Yourself in the Desire

See, hear, taste, touch and feel with your imagination yourself in the desire.

4   Feel the Feeling of an Ideal Outcome

Even if you have no idea how it came about!

5   Feel the Emotions to Their Maximum Effect

Feel it all now regardless. Feel so appreciative for it being received by you.

Enjoying the feeling, then off to enjoy your day and follow what feels fun!

Notes

Q&A

How often would you recommend practicing the visualisation?
Once everyday during week two and three, for as long as it feels good - whether that's a minute or five minutes.

I'm getting pulled out of the moment by reading, do you have an audio of the visualisation I can listen to?
Yes! The audio format of the vibrational harmony visualisation is available to download from soulsparkjournal.com/vhv-audio

What if my visualisation doesn't feel good, but feels negative?
If it feels negative, you're activating the absence of the desire. This could simply be in the visualisation, you're thinking you really want this, but you don't know how to make it yours. Maybe you're feeling the fear of never having this, jealousy for others who have it or doubt it could ever be yours. These feelings are all very common, and simply mean the visualisation is activating the absence of the desire - It's just a signal you're pointed in the wrong direction!

As you focus, you activate the frequency of what that desire or object represents to you and you feel a corresponding emotion. Then as you keep focusing and feeling, the law of attraction will bring to you thoughts and memories that match that same frequency.

So if an aspect of your visualisation feel negative, ditch focusing on that aspect! Pivot and select a different aspect.

Does it feel positive? Awesome! What is that specific emotion?
What are aspects of this desire that feel good to focus on?
Keep that feeling focused in the front of mind. Keep it simple and feel it to the best of your ability.

If, as you practise the visualisation, your mind starts
highlighting why this couldn't possibly come about or be true for you; you
might like to complete the following exercise 'disputing a belief'

It can seem easier to push these thoughts aside in the moment and try and
ignore them, but they may fester in the background. After all, the law of attraction
brings to us predominantly what we're feeling, not just what we're thinking. It can be
very effective to address these and use your mind productively to disprove these
doubtful thoughts!

Why couldn't this possibly come about for me?

....

....

....

....

....

Try to restate this into a concise sentence starting with 'I'

(e.g. I can have love or money but not both)

....

....

Can I recognise that this 'point of view' is based on a limited set of data?

....

....

....

....

Can I collect facts from other people that disputes this?

....
....
....
....

Can I collect facts from other sources that dispute this?

....
....
....
....
....

Turn the statement around

(e.g. I can have love __and__ money)

....
....

Which perspective would I like to adopt going forward?

(e.g. love and money is available to me and my partner)

....
....
....
....

Notes

Notes

ENERGY CHECK IN

What am I feeling not-so-good about?

....

....

....

....

....

....

....

....

....

....

....

....

....

....

....

....

....

....

....

....

....

....

How would I like to feel?

How can I move towards this?

....

....

....

....

....

....

....

....

....

....

....

....

....

....

....

....

....

....

....

....

ACT AS IF

Magnify the Vibration of Your Desire by Embodying It in Your Life

~

"The quality of this moment is the most important point
of creation. Every thought you think and every choice you
make in this moment is setting your future in motion."
–Louise Hay

Continue to practise visualising and feeling your desire,
and magnify it by acting as if this is who you already are!
We're building upon the feelings of having already received
our desire, to acting as if it's already in our lives.

How would I imagine someone who has this desire...
If you're not sure, just imagine and make it up!
...thinks and feels about this?

....

....

....

....

....

....

... speaks to themselves and speaks to others about this?

....

....

....

....

....

....

... carries themselves?

....

....

....

....

....

....

... goes about their day?

How is this different from how I currently think, speak and act?

Vibrational Harmony Visualisation

Practise the Vibrational Harmony Visualisation daily during this week,
for as long as it feels good for you!
You're welcome to listen to the audio format by downloading it from
sculsparkjournal.com/vhv-audio

1   Connect to your heart

*Shift your focus to the area of your heart, and slowly inhale and exhale.
After a few breaths, feel the feeling of appreciation for anything or anyone,
to the best of your ability.*

2   Think of your clear specific desire

Focus on this for a few seconds ... 17 seconds

3   Visualise yourself in the desire.

See, hear, taste, touch and feel with your imagination yourself in the desire.

4   Feel the feeling of an ideal outcome

Even if you have no idea how it came about!

5   Feel it to the best of your ability, to the maximum effect!

Feel it all now regardless. Feel so appreciative for it being received by you.

Enjoying the feeling, then off to enjoy your day and follow what feels fun!

If I imagine someone who already has this desire,

 Is there something they consistently do to maintain having this in their lives?

...everyday

....

....

....

....

....

....

... every week

....

....

....

....

....

....

... every month

....

....

....

....

....

If this desire was already in my life, what things would I do differently?

....

....

....

....

....

....

....

....

....

....

....

....

....

....

....

....

....

....

....

....

....

....

Imagine you are an actor and you're going to embody the best version of yourself and that your desire is a done deal!

How would I act?

....
....
....
....
....
....
....
....
....

What would my day be like?

....
....
....
....
....
....
....
....
....
....
....

Imagine you are an actor and you're going to embody the best version of yourself and that your desire is a done deal!

How is my body language?

....

....

....

....

....

....

....

....

....

How is my tone?

....

....

....

....

....

....

....

....

....

....

Which of these characteristics could I choose to fully embrace?

....

....

....

....

....

....

....

....

....

....

....

....

....

....

....

....

....

....

....

....

....

....

....

Do I have concerns about embracing these parts of myself?

How does my inner guidance feel about these concerns?

....
....
....
....
....
....
....
....
....
....
....
....
....
....
....
....
....
....
....
....
....
....
....
....

What could I start incorporating that will empower me to
move forward?

From this place of acting as if my desire is a done-deal,
what am I excited to do?

....

....

....

....

....

....

....

....

....

....

....

....

....

....

....

....

....

....

....

Practise those in your days!

Notes

As you follow the guided process to manifest your desires, if your mind starts highlighting why this couldn't possibly come about or be true for you; you might like to complete this disputing a thought pattern exercise.

It can seem easier to push these thoughts aside in the moment and try and ignore them, but they may fester in the background. After all, the law of attraction brings to us predominantly what we're feeling, not just what we're thinking. I believe it's more effective to address these head on and use our mind

Why couldn't this possibly come about for me?

....

....

....

....

....

Try to restate this into a concise sentence starting with 'I'

(e.g. I can have love _or_ money but not both)

....

....

Can I recognise that this 'point of view' is based on a limited set of data?

....

....

....

....

Can I collect facts from other people that disputes this?

....

....

....

....

Can I collect facts from other sources that dispute this?

....

....

....

....

....

Turn the statement around

(e.g. I can have love _and_ money)

....

....

Which perspective would I like to adopt going forward?

(e.g. love and money is available to me and my partner)

....

....

....

....

Let Go of Your Attachment and Move Forward in Peace

～

"Risk being seen for all of your glory. You are ready and
able to do beautiful things in this world."
–Jim Carrey

Let go of the need to know how it will all come about; allowing you
to move forward in peace. Letting go creates space. And it's this space
that all the magic can fit in and express itself. Allow your desire to be
revealed in the exciting ways that they will!

Am I using action to compensate for misaligned feelings and
energy?

....

....

....

....

....

....

....

....

....

What am I doing to make this desire come about?
Through my action, time and energy

....

....

....

....

....

....

....

....

How does it feel when I take these actions?

Is it uplifting and fun? Or does it feel like a burden and deflating...

Letting Go

*Practice letting go and moving forward in peace
by reading this script to yourself daily during this week.*

66

From this day-
I commit to stop analysing why things perhaps haven't gone better as they relate to this desire, and instead, I choose to let go and let them be better!

I allow all to be revealed, and I'm excited in the ways that they will! And in doing so, I give myself permission to feel good now, to feel how I want to feel regardless of when or how this comes into my life.

I choose to let go of trying to control the 'how' how it will all come about, and I'm choosing to let go of my attachment to this desire.

I'm deciding to no longer compensate for misaligned energy by offering more time or action. Just like a helpful assistant taking care of all of the details in the background, I trust that my desire is coming to me all in perfect timing. and I trust that if something is required of me, I will feel the intuitive nudge that will bring it to my attention.

I choose to move forward in a state of peace, taking action when it feels great to do so from a place of intention.

I let go of my need to know how it will all come about. I know that letting go creates space. And it's this space that all of the magic can flow in and express itself. I gently flow with life and each new experience. I appreciate where I am, I'm so grateful, I'm excited and eager as things unfold and get better and better!

99

Am I holding on to a reality so tightly that I'm limiting this manifestation coming in unexpected ways?

....

....

....

....

....

....

....

....

....

....

....

....

....

....

....

....

....

....

....

....

....

....

Can I acknowledge that the universe might have something better
in store for me than I can conceive of right now?
Something more enjoyable and in alignment with my highest good

....
....
....
....
....
....
....
....
....
....
....
....
....
....
....
....
....
....
....
....

How might I let go of any chronic longing, whilst still keeping the
faith that my desire will show up in divine timing?

....

....

....

....

....

....

....

....

....

....

....

....

....

....

....

....

....

....

....

....

....

....

....

....

How can I trust in the flow of life?

....

....

....

....

....

....

....

....

....

....

....

....

....

....

....

....

....

....

....

....

Notes

Notes

Notes

....

....

....

....

....

....

....

....

....

....

....

....

....

....

....

....

....

....

....

....

....

....

....

....

Notes

THE UNIVERSE ONLY EVER HAS 3 ANSWERS:

1   Yes

2   Not right now

3   I have something better in store for you

Select a Singular Desire You'd Love to Manifest

~

"Don't be afraid about failures, worry about the chances
you miss when you don't even try."
–Jack Canfeild

Here you get to choose one desire you'd love to manifest.
You can start by brainstorming ideas of what you'd love to be, do or
have. Have fun with this and allow yourself to consider what would
light you up!

What singular desire would I love to manifest?

Sometimes we know exactly what we want!
Start by brainstorming ideas of what you'd love to be, do or have.

....

....

....

....

....

....

....

....

....

....

....

....

....

....

....

....

....

....

....

....

....

....

What would be a game changer?

*Could it be an experience, a lifestyle change, an item you've always
wanted, or simply a state of being and feeling.*

....

....

....

....

....

....

....

....

....

What have I been wanting... but denying?

*Sometimes we do know what we want... but we deny it, push it down, because
we don't know how to get it, don't feel worthy of it, or just don't want to get
excited only to be disappointed if it doesn't come about.*

....

....

....

....

....

....

....

....

....

Sometimes, we honestly don't know what we want.

Maybe our needs haven't been first in line for a long time, or because we haven't given ourselves the chance to consider what we even want, or we just haven't imagined anything other then our current reality, and we're out of inspiration. If you're not sure about what you want, it's helpful to first define what you don't want.

What don't I want?

....

....

....

....

....

....

....

....

....

....

....

....

....

....

....

....

....

....

Next to each item you no longer want to experience, write the opposite.

What do I want instead?

....

....

....

....

....

....

....

....

....

....

....

....

....

....

....

....

....

....

....

....

....

....

What do I need more of in my life?

....

....

....

....

....

....

....

....

....

What do I need less of in my life?

....

....

....

....

....

....

....

....

....

....

What do I feel influenced to go after right now?

....

....

....

....

....

....

....

....

....

....

Do I actually want to pursue any of these, or are they someone else's
expectation of what I should want?

....

....

....

....

....

....

....

....

....

....

....

....

Treat Pinterest like a shopping catalogue for inspiration!
Save some images you're drawn too in a dedicated soulspark board. Once you've gone on a pinning spree, have a look to see if there are any similaritie.

Are there any similarities between these images?
What images are you drawn to?
Maybe the similarities are people, friends, family, connection and love.
Is there a certain vibe that you're loving? Is it certain emotions that are similar?
These similarities in the images you've pinned will likely convey desires and aspects you'd like to integrate into your life.

....

....

....

....

....

....

....

....

....

....

....

....

....

....

....

....

In my heart, what do I really truly want to be, do or have?

....

....

....

....

....

....

....

....

....

....

....

....

....

....

....

....

....

....

....

....

....

....

....

Which area in my life needs the most care and attention right now?

....

....

....

....

....

....

....

....

....

....

....

....

....

....

....

....

....

....

....

....

....

....

....

....

All desires and ideas I've brainstormed!

List out all the ideas of that you'd love to be, do or have based on today's excises

....

....

....

....

....

....

....

....

....

....

....

....

....

....

....

....

....

....

....

....

....

....

....

....

Choose a singular desire from the list that you'd love to manifest?

....

....

....

....

....

....

....

....

....

My desire is ...

....

....

....

....

....

....

....

....

....

Notes

....

....

....

....

....

....

....

....

....

....

....

....

....

....

....

....

....

....

....

....

....

....

Get Clear on Your Desire's Specific Aspects

"Don't ask yourself what the world needs, ask yourself what
makes you come alive. And then go and do that. Because
what the world needs is people who have come alive."
–Harold Whitman

Define the aspects of this desire that important to you. Allow yourself
to consider, without limitation, what does this desire look like and
how does it feel.

Focus on the why - Why do I want this desire?

....

....

....

....

....

....

....

....

....

We usually want something because we believe we will feel better having it.

How do I think I would feel if I had this desire?

....

....

....

....

....

....

....

....

....

....

....

....

If you could wave a wand and change your current reality
as it relates to this desire,
How would you like things to be different?

....

....

....

....

....

....

....

....

....

....

....

....

....

....

....

....

....

....

....

....

....

....

What aspects of this desire are important to me?
(even if I have no idea how these could come about)

....

....

....

....

....

....

....

....

....

What am I not willing to give up in order to receive this desire?
These are your terms!

....

....

....

....

....

....

....

....

....

....

....

I like the idea of this desire overall

I like these aspects:

....
- ....
- ....
- ....
- ....
- ....
- ....
- ....
- ....

I don't like these aspects:

....
- ....
- ....
- ....
- ....
- ....
- ....
- ....
- ....
- ....

What does this desire look like?

Have a clear picture. If I were describing a photo of this desire, what would it look like? Don't limit yourself here, get excited, let your imagination run wild!

....

....

....

....

....

....

....

....

....

....

....

....

....

....

....

....

....

....

....

....

....

....

Remember, your choice of words are important in evoking the desired feeling and frequency

My desire,   looks like:

....

....
- ....
- ....
- ....
- ....
- ....
- ....

My desire,   feels like:

....
- ....
- ....
- ....
- ....
- ....
- ....
- ....
- ....
- ....

My desire,

looks like

and feels like

Notes

Exercise

TAKE IT FURTHER BY CREATING A VISION BOARD

You might like to create vision board for your desire!
Here are some ideas:

Create a physical vision board for your desire, using a pin board
or decorative frame and hang it in your space.

Get creative and use the next few pages as a place to draw, scrapbook
or collage aspects of your desire.

Create a digital vision board and save the image as your laptop
and/or phone wallpaper. Visit soulsparkjournal.com/vision-board
to download our digital vision board resources.

If you're feeling really savvy, you could even create a moving image
video vision board and overlay a favourite song that enhances the
visuals.

Notes

....

....

....

....

....

....

....

....

....

....

....

....

....

....

....

....

....

....

....

....

....

....

....

Become a Vibration Match by Feeling the Corresponding Emotions

~

"Within you is a divine capacity to manifest and
attract all that you need or desire."
–Wayne Dyer

You've identified your singular focus, what it looks like and what it
feels like Now it's time to feel those emotions now,
to the best of your ability, regardless!

Why do I want this desire? What would this mean to me?
Amp-up the heart-felt emotion of this desire. Ask yourself why do you want the
desire until you get to a really good feeing.

....

....

....

....

....

....

....

....

....

....

....

....

....

....

....

....

....

....

....

....

....

How does my inner guidance feel about this desire?

Intention + Heartfelt Emotion

On the following page is the visualisation ritual I felt inspired to craft to deliberately and most effectively place ourselves in a vibrational place of receiving all that we're asking for.

You're welcome to listen to the audio format by downloading it from soulsparkjournal.com/vhv-audio

Practise the Vibrational Harmony Visualisation daily during this week, for as long as it feels good for you!

And if you're interested in diving in deeper, here's how it works...

First, connecting with your heart decreases stress and anxiety and signals that your body is safe. When your heart beats in synchrony with the energy of appreciation, it harmonises the heart and mind into to a cohesive rhythm.

Visualising yourself in your desire is a powerful way to create a feeling of what you want. As you focus, you activate the frequency of what that desire or object represents to you and you feel that corresponding emotion.

When you activate a feeling, you can literally feel the energetic momentum. The exciting part is that the first manifestation you'll receive is the *feeling*.

Feeling those emotions of your ideal outcome, to the best of your ability helps you to ease any discomfort of how it all might be received - separating your thoughts from the past, and away from others experiences, towards your new reality.

All infinite possibilities exist in the quantum field. When we allow ourselves to be immersed into this visualisation, we're collapsing those possibilities of a wave, into a particle - using the power of our intention plus heartfelt emotion to create our new reality!

Practise the Vibrational Harmony Visualisation daily during this week, for as long as it feels good for you!

"Everything is energy and that's all there is to it. Match the frequency of the reality you want and you cannot help but get that reality. It can be no other way. This is not philosophy. This is physics."

–Albert Einstein

Vibrational Harmony Visualisation

It can be uncomfortable for our mind to go places that are unfamiliar, so you might
like to start with a disclaimer to your mind —
"I'm trying something new and it's probably going to feel a little odd and strange
because it's unfamiliar. But, I'm choosing to do this and I ask my mind to go along
with this experiment and adventure. Please suspend all doubt and disbelief for a
month and let's just see what happens!"

1   Connect to Your Heart

Shift your focus to the area of your heart, and slowly inhale and exhale.
After a few breaths, feel the feeling of appreciation for anything or anyone,
to the best of your ability.

2   Think of Your Clear Specific Desire

Focus on this for a few seconds ... 17 seconds

3   Visualise Yourself in the Desire

See, hear, taste, touch and feel with your imagination yourself in the desire.

4   Feel the Feeling of an Ideal Outcome

Even if you have no idea how it came about!

5   Feel the Emotions to Their Maximum Effect

Feel it all now regardless. Feel so appreciative for it being received by you.

Enjoying the feeling, then off to enjoy your day and follow what feels fun!

Notes

....

....

....

....

....

....

....

....

....

....

....

....

....

....

....

....

....

....

....

....

....

....

....

Q&A

How often would you recommend practicing the visualisation?
Once everyday during week two and three, for as long as it feels good - whether that's a minute or five minutes.

I'm getting pulled out of the moment by reading, do you have an audio of the visualisation I can listen to?
Yes! The audio format of the vibrational harmony visualisation is available to download from soulsparkjournal.com/vhv-audio

What if my visualisation doesn't feel good, but feels negative?
If it feels negative, you're activating the absence of the desire. This could simply be in the visualisation, you're thinking you really want this, but you don't know how to make it yours. Maybe you're feeling the fear of never having this, jealousy for others who have it or doubt it could ever be yours. These feelings are all very common, and simply mean the visualisation is activating the absence of the desire - It's just a signal you're pointed in the wrong direction!

As you focus, you activate the frequency of what that desire or object represents to you and you feel a corresponding emotion. Then as you keep focusing and feeling, the law of attraction will bring to you thoughts and memories that match that same frequency.

So if an aspect of your visualisation feel negative, ditch focusing on that aspect! Pivot and select a different aspect.

Does it feel positive? Awesome! What is that specific emotion?
What are aspects of this desire that feel good to focus on?
Keep that feeling focused in the front of mind. Keep it simple and feel it to the best of your ability.

If, as you practise the visualisation, your mind starts
highlighting why this couldn't possibly come about or be true for you; you
might like to complete the following exercise 'disputing a belief'

It can seem easier to push these thoughts aside in the moment and try and
ignore them, but they may fester in the background. After all, the law of attraction
brings to us predominantly what we're feeling, not just what we're thinking. It can be
very effective to address these and use your mind productively to disprove these
doubtful thoughts!

Why couldn't this possibly come about for me?

....

....

....

....

....

Try to restate this into a concise sentence starting with 'I'

(e.g. I can have love _or_ money but not both)

....

....

Can I recognise that this 'point of view' is based on a limited set of data?

....

....

....

....

Can I collect facts from other people that disputes this?

....

....

....

....

Can I collect facts from other sources that dispute this?

....

....

....

....

....

Turn the statement around

(e.g. I can have love _and_ money)

....

....

Which perspective would I like to adopt going forward?

(e.g. love and money is available to me and my partner)

....

....

....

....

Notes

....

....

....

....

....

....

....

....

....

....

....

....

....

....

....

....

....

....

....

....

....

....

....

Notes

ENERGY CHECK IN

What am I feeling not-so-good about?

How would I like to feel?

How can I move towards this?

Magnify the Vibration of Your Desire by Embodying It in Your Life

"We encourage you to decide, as early in life as possible,
that your dominant intent and reason for existence
is to live happily ever after."
–Abraham Hicks

Continue to practise visualising and feeling your desire,
and magnify it by acting as if this is who you already are!
We're building upon the feelings of having already received
our desire, to acting as if it's already in our lives.

How would I imagine someone who has this desire...
If you're not sure, just imagine and make it up!
...thinks and feels about this?

....

....

....

....

....

....

... speaks to themselves and speaks to others about this?

....

....

....

....

....

....

... carries themselves?

....

....

....

....

....

....

... goes about their day?

....
....
....
....
....
....
....

How is this different from how I currently think, speak and act?

....
....
....
....
....
....
....
....
....
....
....
....
....
....

Vibrational Harmony Visualisation

Practise the Vibrational Harmony Visualisation daily during this week,
for as long as it feels good for you!
You're welcome to listen to the audio format by downloading it from
soulsparkjournal.com/vhv-audio

1   Connect to your heart

*Shift your focus to the area of your heart, and slowly inhale and exhale.
After a few breaths, feel the feeling of appreciation for anything or anyone,
to the best of your ability.*

2   Think of your clear specific desire

Focus on this for a few seconds ... 17 seconds

3   Visualise yourself in the desire.

See, hear, taste, touch and feel with your imagination yourself in the desire.

4   Feel the feeling of an ideal outcome

Even if you have no idea how it came about!

5   Feel it to the best of your ability, to the maximum effect!

Feel it all now regardless. Feel so appreciative for it being received by you.

Enjoying the feeling then off to enjoy your day and follow what feels fun!

If I imagine someone who already has this desire,

 Is there something they consistently do to maintain having this in their lives?

...everyday

....

....

....

....

....

....

... every week

....

....

....

....

....

....

... every month

....

....

....

....

....

If this desire was already in my life, what things would I do differently?

....

....

....

....

....

....

....

....

....

....

....

....

....

....

....

....

....

....

....

....

....

Imagine you are an actor and you're going to embody the best version of yourself and that your desire is a done deal!

How would I act?

....

....

....

....

....

....

....

....

What would my day be like?

....

....

....

....

....

....

....

....

....

....

Imagine you are an actor and you're going to embody the best version of yourself and that your desire is a done deal!

How is my body language?

....

....

....

....

....

....

....

....

....

How is my tone?

....

....

....

....

....

....

....

....

....

....

Which of these characteristics could I choose to fully embrace?

....

....

....

....

....

....

....

....

....

....

....

....

....

....

....

....

....

....

....

....

Do I have concerns about embracing these parts of myself?

....

....

....

....

....

....

....

....

....

....

....

....

....

....

....

....

....

....

....

....

How does my inner guidance feel about these concerns?

What could I start incorporating that will empower me to
move forward?

....
....
....
....
....
....
....
....
....
....
....
....
....
....
....
....
....
....
....
....
....
....

From this place of acting as if my desire is a done-deal,
what am I excited to do?

....

....

....

....

....

....

....

....

....

....

....

....

....

....

....

....

....

....

....

Practise those in your days!

Notes

As you follow the guided process to manifest your desires, if your mind starts highlighting why this couldn't possibly come about or be true for you; you might like to complete this disputing a thought pattern exercise.

It can seem easier to push these thoughts aside in the moment and try and ignore them, but they may fester in the background. After all, the law of attraction brings to us predominantly what we're feeling, not just what we're thinking. I believe it's more effective to address these head on and use our mind

Why couldn't this possibly come about for me?

....

....

....

....

....

Try to restate this into a concise sentence starting with 'I'

(e.g. I can have love _or_ money but not both)

....

....

Can I recognise that this 'point of view' is based on a limited set of data?

....

....

....

....

Can I collect facts from other people that disputes this?

....

....

....

....

Can I collect facts from other sources that dispute this?

....

....

....

....

....

Turn the statement around

(e.g. I can have love _and_ money)

....

....

Which perspective would I like to adopt going forward?

(e.g. love and money is available to me and my partner)

....

....

....

....

Let Go of Your Attachment and Move Forward in Peace

~

"It is not your role to fix the feeling of lack within others; it is your role to keep yourself in balance. You only ever uplift from your position of strength and clarity and alignment."
–Abraham Hicks

Let go of the need to know how it will all come about; allowing you to move forward in peace. Letting go creates space. And it's this space that all the magic can fit in and express itself. Allow your desire to be revealed in the exciting ways that they will!

Am I using action to compensate for misaligned feelings and
energy?

....

....

....

....

....

....

....

....

....

What am I doing to make this desire come about?
Through my action, time and energy

....

....

....

....

....

....

....

....

....

How does it feel when I take these actions?

Is it uplifting and fun? Or does it feel like a burden and deflating...

Letting Go

*Practice letting go and moving forward in peace
by reading this script to yourself daily during this week.*

"

From this day-
I commit to stop analysing why things perhaps haven't gone better as they relate to this desire, and instead, I choose to let go and let them be better!

I allow all to be revealed, and I'm excited in the ways that they will! And in doing so, I give myself permission to feel good now, to feel how I want to feel regardless of when or how this comes into my life.

I choose to let go of trying to control the 'how' how it will all come about, and I'm choosing to let go of my attachment to this desire.

I'm deciding to no longer compensate for misaligned energy by offering more time or action. Just like a helpful assistant taking care of all of the details in the background, I trust that my desire is coming to me all in perfect timing, and I trust that if something is required of me, I will feel the intuitive nudge that will bring it to my attention.

I choose to move forward in a state of peace, taking action when it feels great to do so from a place of intention.

I let go of my need to know how it will all come about. I know that letting go creates space. And it's this space that all of the magic can flow in and express itself. I gently flow with life and each new experience. I appreciate where I am, I'm so grateful, I'm excited and eager as things unfold and get better and better!

"

Am I holding on to a reality so tightly that I'm limiting this
manifestation coming in unexpected ways?

....

....

....

....

....

....

....

....

....

....

....

....

....

....

....

....

....

....

....

....

Can I acknowledge that the universe might have something better
in store for me that I can conceive of right now?
Something more enjoyable and in alignment with my highest good

....
....
....
....
....
....
....
....
....
....
....
....
....
....
....
....
....
....
....
....

How might I let go of any chronic longing, whilst still keeping the
faith that my desire will show up in divine timing?

....

....

....

....

....

....

....

....

....

....

....

....

....

....

....

....

....

....

....

....

How can I trust in the flow of life?

Notes

....

....

....

....

....

....

....

....

....

....

....

....

....

....

....

....

....

....

....

....

....

....

....

....

Notes

Observations · Precursors · Manifestations
Here we're recognising and building momentum–
Feel free to use these spaces to recognise the small wins, the synchronicities and to
celebrate and document your manifestations!

....

....

....

....

....

....

....

....

....

....

....

....

....

....

....

....

....

....

....

....

....

....

Observations · Precurers · Manifestations
Here we're recognizing and building momentum–
Feel free to use these spaces to recognise the small wins, the sincrinities
and to celebrate and document your manifestations!

....

....

....

....

....

....

....

....

....

....

....

....

....

....

....

....

....

....

....

....